THE
Mirror of Alchemy,

Composed by the thrice-famous and learned
Frier, *Roger Bacon*, sometimes fellow of
Martin College: and afterwards of
Brasen-nose College in
Oxenforde.

With the Smaragdine Table of *Hermes,*
Trismegistus of Alchemy.

Vino vendibili non opus est hedera.

LOS ANGELES
1975

The Preface

 N times past the Philosophers spoke after diverse and sundry manners throughout their writings, such that as it were in a riddle and cloudy voice, they have left unto us a certain most excellent and noble science, but altogether obscure, and without all hope utterly denied, and that not without good cause. Wherefore I would advise you, that above all other books, you should firmly fix your mind upon these seven Chapters, containing in them the transmutation of metals, and often call to mind the beginning, middle, and end of the same, wherein you will find such subtility, that your mind will be fully contented therewith.

The

The Mirror of Alche-

my, composed by the famous Frier,
Roger Bacon, sometime fellow of
Martin College and *Brasen-nose*
College in *Oxenforde.*

CHAP. I.

Of the Definitions of Alchemy.

N many ancient Books there are found many definitions of this Art, the intentions whereof we must consider in this Chapter. For *Hermes* said of this Science: *Alchemy* is a Corporal Science simply composed of one and by one, naturally conjoining things more precious, by knowledge and effect, and converting them by a natural commixtion into a better kind. A certain other said: *Alchemy* is a Science, teaching how to transform any kind of metal into another: and that by a proper medicine, as it appeared by many Philosophers' Books. *Alchemy* therefore is a science teaching how to make and compound a certain medicine, which is called *Elixir,* the which when it is cast upon metals or imperfect bodies, does fully perfect them in the very projection.

CHAP.

CHAP. II.

Of the natural principles, and procreation of Minerals.

SEcondly, I will perfectly declare the natural principles & procreations of Minerals: where first it is to be noted, that the natural principles in the mines, are *Argent-vive*, and *Sulphur*. All metals and minerals, whereof there be sundry and diverse kinds, are begotten of these two: but I must tell you, that nature always intends and strives to the perfection of Gold: but many accidents coming between, change the metals, as it is evidently to be seen in diverse of the Philosophers books. For according to the purity and impurity of the two aforesaid principles, *Argent-vive*, and *Sulphur*, pure, and impure metals are engendered: to wit, Gold, Silver, Steel, Lead, Copper, and Iron: of whose nature, that is to say, purity, and impurity, or unclean superfluity and defect, give ear to that which follows.

Of the nature of Gold.

GOld is a perfect body, engendered of *Argent-vive* pure, fixed, clear, red, and of *Sulphur* clean, fixed, red, not burning, and it wants nothing.

Of the nature of Silver.

SIlver is a body, clean, pure, and almost perfect, begotten of *Argent-vive*, pure, almost fixed, clear, and white,

&

& of such a like *Sulphur:* It wants nothing, save a little fixation, color, and weight.

Of the nature of Steel.

STeel is a body clean, imperfect, engendered of Argent-vive pure, fixed & not fixed clear, white outwardly, but red inwardly, and of the like Sulphur. It wants only decoction or digestion.

Of the nature of Lead.

LEad is an unclean and imperfect body, engendered of Argent-vive impure, not fixed, earthy, drossy, somewhat white outwardly, and red inwardly, and of such a Sulphur in part burning. It wants purity, fixation, color, and firing.

Of the nature of Copper.

COpper is an unclean and imperfect body, engendered of Argent-vive, impure, not fixed, earthy, burning, red not clear, and of the like Sulphur. It wants purity, fixation, and weight: and has too much of an impure color, and earthiness not burning.

Of the nature Iron.

IRon is an unclean and imperfect body, engendered of Argent-vive impure, too much fixed, earthy, burning, white and red not clear, and of the like Sulphur: It wants fusion, purity, and weight: It has too much fixed unclean Sulphur, and burning earthiness. That which

which has been spoken, every Alchemist must diligently observe.

CHAP. III.

Out of what things the matter of Elixir must be more nearly extracted.

THe generation of metals, as well perfect, as imperfect, is sufficiently declared by that which has been already spoken. Now let us return to the imperfect matter that must be chosen and made perfect. Seeing that by the former Chapters we have been taught, that all metals are engendered of Argent-vive and Sulphur, and how that their impurity and uncleanness does corrupt, and that nothing may be mingled with metals which have not been made or sprung from them, it remains clean enough, that no strange thing which has not his original from these two, is able to perfect them, or to make a change and new transmutation of them: so that it is to be wondered at, that any wise man should set his mind upon living creatures, or vegetables which are far off, when there be minerals to be found near enough: neither may we in any way think, that any of the Philosophers placed the Art in the said remote things, except it were by way of comparison: but of the aforesaid two, all metals are made, neither does any thing cleave unto them or is joined with them, not yet changes them, but that which is of them, and so of right we must take

Argent-

Argent-vive and Sulphur for the matter of our stone:
Neither does Argent-vive by itself alone, nor Sulphur by
itself alone, beget any metal, but of the commixtion of
them both, diverse metals and minerals are diversely
brought forth. Our matter therefore must be chosen of
the commixtion of them both: but our final secret is
most excellent, and most hidden, to wit, of what mineral thing that is more near than others, it should be made:
and in making choice hereof, we must be very wary. I
put the case then, if our matter were first of all drawn out
of vegetables, (of which sort are herbs, trees, and what-
soever springs out of the earth) here we must first make
Argent-vive & Sulphur. by a long decoction, from which
things, and their operation we are excused: for nature
herself offers unto us Argent-vive and Sulphur. And if
we should draw it from living creatures (of which sort is
man's blood, hair, urine, excrements, hens' eggs, and
what else proceed from living creatures) we must likewise
out of them extract Argent-vive and Sulphur by decoction, from which we are freed, as we were before. Or if
we should choose it out of middle minerals (of which
sort are all kinds of *Magnesia*, *Marchasites*, of *Tutia*,
Coppers, Allums, Baurach, Salts, and many other) we
should likewise, as afore, extract Argent-vive and Sulphur by decoction: from which as from the former, we
are also excused. And if we should take one of the
seven spirits by itself. as Argent-vive, or Sulphur alone,
or Argent-vive and one of the two Sulphurs, or Sulphur-

vive

vive, or Auripigment, or Citrine Arsenicum, or red alone, or the like: we should never effect it, because since nature does never perfect anything without equal commixtion of both, neither can we: from these therefore, as from the foresaid Argent-vive and Sulphur in their nature we are excused. Finally, if we should choose them, we should mix everything as it is, according to a due proportion, which no man knows, and afterward decoct it to coagulation, into a solid lump: and therefore we are excused from receiving both of them in their proper nature: to wit, Argent-vive and Sulphur, seeing we know not their proportion, and that we may meet with bodies, wherein we shall find the said things proportioned, coagulated & gathered together, after a due manner. Keep this secret more secretly. Gold is a perfect masculine body, without any superfluity or diminution: and if it should perfect imperfect bodies mingled with it by melting only, it should be Elixir to red. Silver is also a body almost perfect, and feminine, which if it should almost perfect imperfect bodies by his common melting only, it should be Elixir to white which it is not, nor cannot be, because they only are perfect. And if this perfection might be mixed with the imperfect, the imperfect should not be perfected with the perfect, but rather their perfections should be diminished by the imperfect, & become imperfect. But if they were more than perfect, either in a two-fold, four-fold, hundred-fold, or larger proportion, they
might

might then well perfect the imperfect. And forasmuch as nature does always work simply, the perfection which is in them is simple, inseparable, & incommiscible, neither may they by art be put in the stone, for ferment to shorten the work, and so brought to their former state, because the most volatile does overcome the most fixed. And for that gold is a perfect body, consisting of Argent-vive, red and clear, & of such a Sulphur, therefore we choose it not for the matter of our stone to the red Elixir, because it is so simply perfect, without artificial mundification, & so strongly digested and fed with a natural heat, that with our artificial fire, we are scarcely able to work on gold or silver. And though nature does perfect anything, yet she cannot thoroughly mundify, or perfect and purify it, because she simply works on that which she has. If therefore we should choose gold or silver for the matter of the stone, we should hard and scantly find fire working in them. And although we are not ignorant of the fire, yet could we not come to the thorough mundification & perfection of it, by reason of his most firm knitting together, and natural composition: we are therefore excused for taking the first too red, or the second too white, seeing we may find out a thing or some body of as clean, or rather more clean Sulphur & Argent-vive, on which nature has wrought little or nothing at all, which with our artificial fire, & experience of our art, we are able to bring unto his due concoction, mundification, color

and

and fixation, continuing our ingenious labor upon it. There must therefore be such a matter chosen, where in there is Argent-vive, clean, pure, clear, white & red, not fully complete, but equally and proportionably commixt after a due manner with the like Sulphur, & congealed into a solid mass, that by our wisdom and discretion, and by our artificial fire, we may attain unto the uttermost cleanness of it, and the purity of the same, and bring it to that pass, that after the work ended, it might be a thousand thousand times more strong and perfect, then the simple bodies themselves, decoct by their natural heat. Be therefore wise: for if you shall be subtle and witty in my Chapters (wherein by manifest prose I have laid open the matter of the stone easy to be known) you shall taste of that delightful thing, wherein the whole intention of the Philosophers is placed.

CHAP. IIII.

Of the manner of working, and of moderating,
and continuing the fire.

I hope ere this time you have already found out by the words already spoken (if you are not most dull, ignorant, and foolish) the certain matter of the learned Philosophers blessed stone, whereon *Alchemy* works, while we endeavor to perfect the imperfect, and that with things more then perfect. And for that nature has delivered us the imperfect only with the perfect, it is our

part

part to make the matter (in the former Chapters declared unto us) more then perfect by our artificial labor. And if we know not the manner of working, what is the cause that we do not see how nature (which of long time has perfected metals) does continually work? Do we not see, that in the Mines through the continual heat that is in the mountains thereof, the grossness of water is so decocted & thickened, that in continuance of time it becomes Argent-vive? And that of the fatness of the earth through the same heat and decoction, Sulphur is engendered? And that through the same heat without intermission continued in them, all metals are engendered of them according to their purity and impurity? and that nature does by decoction alone perfect or make all metals, as well perfect as imperfect? O extreme madness! what, I pray you, constrains you to seek to perfect the foresaid things by strange melancholical and fantastical regiments? as one says: Woe to you that will overcome nature, and make metals more then perfect by a new regiment, or work sprung from your own senseless brains. God has given to nature a straight way, to wit, continual concoction, and you like fools despise it, or else know it not. Again, fire and Azot, are sufficient for you. And in another place, Heat perfects all things. And elsewhere, see, see, see, and be not weary. And in another place, let your fire be gentle, & easy, which being always equal, may continue burning: and let it not increase, for if it does,

you

you shall suffer great loss. And in another place, Know you that in one thing, to wit, the stone, by one way, to wit, decoction, and in one vessel the whole mastery is performed. And in another place, patiently, and continually, and in another place, grind it seven times. And in another place, It is ground with fire. And in another place, this work is very like to the creation of man: for as the Infant in the beginning is nourished with light meats, but the bones being strengthened with stronger: so this mastery also, first it must have an easy fire, whereby we must always work in every essence of decoction. And though we always speak of a gentle fire, yet in truth, we think that in governing the work, the fire must always by little and little be increased and augmented unto the end.

CHAP. V.

Of the quality of the Vessel and Furnace.

THe means and manner of working, we have already determined: now we are to speak of the Vessel and Furnace, in what sort, and of what things they must be made. Whereas nature by a natural fire decocts the metals in the Mines, she denies the like decoction to be made without a vessel fit for it. And if we propose to imitate nature in concocting, wherefore do we reject her vessel? Let us first of all therefore, see in what place the generation of metals is made. It does evidently appear in the places of Minerals, that in the

bottom

bottom of the mountain there is heat continually alike, the nature whereof is always to ascend, and in the ascension it always dries up, and coagulates the thicker or grosser water hidden in the belly, or veins of the earth, or mountain, into Argent-vive. And if the mineral fatness of the same place arising out of the earth, be gathered warm together in the veins of the earth, it runs through the mountain, & becomes Sulphur. And as a man may see in the foresaid veins of that place, that Sulphur engendered of the fatness of the earth (as is before touched) meets with the Argent-vive (as it is also written) in the veins of the earth, and begets the thickness of the mineral water. There, through the continual equal heat in the mountain, in long process of time diverse metals are engendered, according to the diversity of the place. And in these Mineral places, you shall find a continual heat. For this cause we are of right to note, that the external mineral mountain is everywhere shut up within itself, and stony: for if the heat might issue out, there should never be engendered any metal. If therefore we intend to immitate nature, we must needs have such a furnace like unto the Mountains, not in greatness, but in continual heat, so that the fire put in, when it ascends, may find no vent: but that the heat may beat upon the vessel being close shut, containing in it the matter of the stone: which vessel must be round, with a small neck, made of glass or some earth, representing the nature or close knitting together of glass: the mouth whereof must be signed or

sealed

sealed with a covering of the same matter, or with lute. And as in the mines, the heat does not immediately touch the matter of Sulphur and Argent-vive, because the earth of the mountain comes everywhere between: So this fire must not immediately touch the vessel, containing the matter of the aforesaid things in it, but it must be put into another vessel, shut closed in the like manner, that so the temperate heat may touch the matter above and beneath, and where ever it be, more aptly and fitly: whereupon *Aristotle* says, in the light of lights, that *Mercury* is to be concocted in a three-fold vessel, and that the vessel must be of most hard Glass, or (which is better) of earth possessing the nature of Glass.

CHAP. VI.

Of the accidental and essential colours appearing in the work.

THe matter of the stone thus ended, you shall know the certain manner of working, by what manner and regiment, the stone is often changed in decoction into diverse colors. Whereupon one says, So many colors, so many names. According to the diverse colors appearing in the work, the names likewise were varied by the Philosophers: whereon, in the first operation of our stone, it is called putrifaction, and our stone is made black: whereof one says, When you find it black, know that in that blackness whiteness is hidden, and you must

extract

extract the same from his most subtle blackness. But after putrifaction it waxes red, not with a true redness, of which one says: It is often red, and often of a citrine color, it often melts, and is often coagulated, before true whiteness. And it dissolves itself, it coagulates it-self, it putrifies itself, it colors itself, it mortifies itself, it quickens itself, it makes itself black, it makes itself white, it makes itself red. It is also green: whereon another says, Concoct it, till it appears green unto you, and that is the soul. And another, Know, that in that green his soul bears dominion. There appears also before whiteness the peacocks color, whereon one says thus, Know you that all the colors in the world, or that may be imagined, appear before whiteness, and afterward true whiteness follows. Whereof one says: When it has been decocted pure and clean, that it shines like the eyes of fishes, then are we to expect his utility, and by that time the stone is congealed round. And another says: When you shall find whiteness atop in the glass, be assured that in that whiteness, redness is hidden: and this you must extract: but concoct it while it becomes all red: for between true whiteness and true redness, there is a certain ash-color: of which it is said, After whiteness, you cannot err, for increasing the fire, you shall come to an ash-color: of which another says: Do not set light by the ashes, for God shall give it to you molten: and then at the last the King is invested with a red crown the by will of God.

CHAP.

CHAP. VII.

*How to make projection of the medicine upon
any imperfect body.*

I Have largely accomplished my promise of that great
mastery, for making the most excellent Elixir, red and
white. For conclusion, we are to treat of the manner of
projection, which is the accomplishment of the work,
the desired and expected joy. The red Elixir turns
into a citrine color infinitely, and changes all metals
into pure gold. And the white Elixir does infinitely
whiten, and brings every metal to perfect whiteness.
But we know that one metal is farther off from perfection then another, & one more near then another. And
although every metal may by Elixir be reduced to perfection, nevertheless the nearest are more easily, speed-
ily, and perfectly reduced, then those which are far dis-
tant. And when we meet with a metal that is near to
perfection, we are thereby excused from many that are
far off. And as for the metals which of them be near,
and which far off, which of them I say be nearest to
perfection, if you are wise and discrete, you shall find
to be plainly and truly set out in my Chapters. And
without doubt, he that is so quick sighted in this my
Mirror, that by his own industry he can find out the
true matter, he does full well know upon what body
the medicine is to be projected to bring it to perfection.
For the forerunners of this Art, who have found it out

by

by their philosophy, do point out with their finger the direct & plain way, when they say: Nature, contains nature: Nature overcomes nature: & Nature meeting with her nature, exceedingly rejoices, and is changed into other natures. And in another place, Every like rejoices in his like: for likeness is said to be the cause of friendship, whereof many Philosophers have left a notable secret. Know you that the soul does quickly enter into his body, which may by no means be joined to another body. And in another place, The soul does quickly enter into his own body, which if you go about to join with another body, you shall loose your labor: for the nearness itself is more clear. And because corporeal things in this regiment are made incorporeal, & contrariwise things incorporeal corporeal, and in the shutting up of the work, the whole body is made a spiritual fixed thing: and because also that spiritual Elixir evidently, whether white or red, is so greatly prepared and decocted beyond his nature, it is no marvel that it cannot be mixed with a body, on which it is projected, being only melted. It is also a hard matter to project it on a thousand thousand and more, and incontinently to penetrate and transmute them. I will therefore now deliver unto you a great and hidden secret. One part is to be mixed with a thousand of the next body, & let all this be surely put into a fit vessel, and set it in a furnace of fixation. first with a lent fire, and afterwards increasing the fire for three days, till
they

they be inseparably joined together, and this is a work of three days: then again and finally every part hereof . by itself, must be projected upon another thousand parts of any near body: and this is a work of one day, or one hour, or a moment, for which our wonderful God is eternally to be praised.

Here ends the Mirror of Alchemy, composed by the most learned Philosopher, Roger Bacon.

The Smaragdine Table

of Hermes, Trismegistus
of Alchemy.

THe words of the secrets of *Hermes*, which were written in a Smaragdine Table, and found between his hands in an obscure vault, wherein his body lay buried. It is true without leasing, certain and most true. That which is beneath is like that which is above: & that which is above, is like that which is beneath, to work the miracles of one thing. And as all things have proceeded from one, by the meditation of one, so all things have sprung from this one thing by adaptation. His father is the sun, his mother is the moon, the wind bore it in her belly. The earth is his nurse. The father of all the telesme of this world is here. His force and power is perfect, if it be turned into earth. Thou shalt separate the earth from the fire, the thin from the thick, and that gently with great discretion. It ascendeth from the Earth into Heaven: and again it descendeth into the earth, and receiveth the power of the superiours and inferiours: so shalt thou have the glory of the whole world. All obscurity therefore shall fly away from thee. This is the mighty power of all power, for it shall overcome every subtle thing, and pierce through every solid thing. So was the world created. Here shall be marvelous adaptations,
whereof

whereof this is the mean. Therefore am I called *Hermes Trismegistus*, or the thrice great Interpreter: having three parts of the Philosophy of the whole world. That which I have spoken of the operation of the Sun, is finished.

Here endeth the Table of Hermes.